**ALL RIGHTS RESERVED**
**Original Works Publishing**

*Harry and the Thief*
© Sigrid Gilmer
Trade Edition, 2018
ISBN 978-1-63092-084-5

## Also Available From
## Original Works Publishing

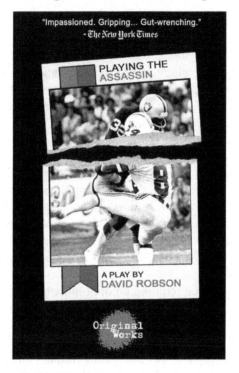

## Playing the Assassin by David Robson

**Synopsis:** In a compelling drama about a man's legacy, former pro football player Frank Baker is offered the chance of a lifetime – an interview on CBS before the Super Bowl. But just when he thinks his luck has changed, Baker and his interviewer are blindsided by secrets and revelations. Inspired by a true story, this new play looks closely at hero worship and forgiveness. How will you be remembered when the final whistle is blown?

**Cast Size:** 2 Males

**"Impassioned. Gripping... Gut-wrenching."**
*—The New York Times*

# HARRY & THE THIEF

## a play by
## Sigrid Gilmer

# PRODUCTION HISTORY

HARRY & THE THIEF was developed in Skylight Theatre Companies (formally The Katselas Theatre Companies) Play-LAb and presented as part of LAB Works 2012, Los Angeles, CA. It was produced by Gary Grossman. Set and lighting design was by Jeff McLaughlin. Sound design by Martin Carrillo. Stage Manager was Christopher Hoffman.

It was directed by Jose Casas. The cast was as follows:

ANITA.  Stephanie Berlanga

MIMI.  Taylor Hawthorne

HARRY.  Kila Kitu

JEREMY.  Kevin Vavassuer

VIVIAN.  Dana L. Wilson

KNOX.  Curtis Tyrone Scott

SHILO.  Tamika Simpkins

MADDOX.  Armond Kinard

ORRY MAIN SCARLET.  Andrew Wright

OVERSEER JONES.  John Collins

4

HARRY & the THIEF was originally produced in 2013 by Pavement Group in Chicago, IL. It was produced by Mary Krupka. Set design was by Megan Truscott. Lighting design by Claire Chrzan. Costume design by Constance Blackmon Lee. Sound design by Jeff Kelley. Props design by Amiee Plant. Choreography by Jenn BeVard. Fight Choreography by Matt Hawkins. Technical direction by Dan Mayer. Stage Manager was Danielle Love. Assistant Director was Elyse Crowles.

It was directed by Krissy Vanderwalker. The cast was as follows:

ANITA. Bryan Bosque

MIMI. Lucy Sandy

HARRY. Marjie Southerland

JEREMY. Osiris Khepera

VIVIAN. McKenzie Chin

KNOX. Tyshaun Lang

SHILO. Morgan McNaught

MADDOX. Manny Buckley

ORRY MAIN SCARLET. Alexander Lang

OVERSEER JONES. Keith Neagle

UNDERSTUDY ORRY/JONES. Jared Fernely
UNDERSTUDY HARRY/SHILO. Krystel McNeil
UNDERSTUDY MIMI/VIVIAN. Sasha Smith
UNDERSTUDY JEREMY/KNOX/MADDOX. Jeremy Sonkins

# CHARACTERS

ANITA. She maybe History. She maybe God. She is most definitely the narrator. She is not black. She is not white. She is not male. She is not female. She is in drag. She is kind of a bitch.

MIMI. Professional thief. Time traveler. Black girl.

HARRY. Harriet Tubman. Her people call her Moses. She's very black. She has a scar on her forehead. She wears a bandana.

JEREMY. Big Black Queen. Mad Scientist. Revolutionary. Full Figured.

BAND (OF SLAVES) ON THE RUN:

VIVIAN. Twin of Knox. Very cute. Very pissed off. She has a baby.

KNOX. Twin of Vivian. He wants to be a cowboy.

SHILO. The Cook. Miss Mary Sunshine with an axe behind her back.

MADDOX. Head Nigger in Charge. Roscoe Lee Brown and John Gielgud's love child.

ORRY MAIN SCARLET. Slave Owner. It's good to be the king. He has a charming southern accent. Handsome.

OVERSEER JONES. He's in love. He looks intimidating.

WHITE MAN WITH A ROCK. Played by Orry Main.

THE VOICES OF:

RONNIE. Played by Knox

BOBBIE. Played by Maddox

RICKY. Played by Jones

MIKE. Played by Orry

**SETTING**

Pasadena, California.
Around Dorchester County, Maryland.
South Carolina.

**TIME**

It's all over the place.
The 1850-60s & NOW

**Notes on tone and style.**

This play is a trunk show. All costumes and set pieces should be done cheaply and stylistically. The playing style is a mix of the easy and heightened swagger of a modern action movie and the camp sensibilities of a civil war epic-think Band of Angels or Gone with the Wind.

It's a terrible thing, simply to be trapped in one's history and attempt in the same motion (and in this our life!) to accept, deny, reject and redeem it - and also on what ever level profit from it.

James Baldwin. *The Devil Finds Work*

# A MOVIE TRAILER FOR A PLAY.

*(The house lights are still on.*

*ANITA enters. She is a zaftig with tons of shiny black hair. She wears a well tailored suit and kick ass heels. She has an old school microphone. It's cord stretches off into infinity.*

*Anita stands at the edge of the space. She scans the audience. She puts the mic to her lips.*

*The space goes black.*

*Two pools of light.*

*In one, HARRY. In the other, shadowed with prison bars, stands MIMI.*

*They are praying.)*

ANITA: *(Speaking in a movie trailer voice.)* Two women.

MIMI: Hi. God. Goddess. Universe. Whatever. I'm even not sure if I believe in you, but-

HARRY: Oh Lord, all powerful merciful Lord, show me the way.

MIMI: I'm in a tight spot.

ANITA: Two different Americas.

HARRY: And I promise you Lord.

MIMI: I pinky swear.

HARRY: I will be your right-         MIMI: I will totally owe
eous servant, forever.                    you, forever.

ANITA: They have only one chance to get it right.

*(Spots out on Mimi and Harry.*

*Lights full. The Scarlet Plantation.*

9

*VIVIAN, a slave, enters. Vivian carries a bundle, it's a baby. Right behind her is KNOX, also a slave.)*

KNOX: I'm not going let you do it.

VIVIAN: You don't own me.

KNOX: It's too dangerous.

VIVIAN: This life is dangerous.

*(Enter OVERSEER JONES. Vivian and Knox are too busy fighting to notice.)*

JONES: *(To Knox.)* Boy, Mr. Scarlet wants his horse. *(To Vivian.)* Morin' Vivian.

*(Jones rubs Vivian's back.*

*Beat. Knox turns to go.*

*Enter SHILO, a slave. She carries a tray. She steps in front of Knox.)*

SHILO: *(To Knox.)* Hoe cake? Mornin' y'all. Aint it a special day?

*(Jones shoves a hoe cake in his mouth.*

*Knox and Vivian reluctantly take one.)*

JONES: They're delicious.

SHILO: I'm glad you approve I made them with my special secret ingredient.

*(Knox & Vivian return the cakes to the tray.*

*ORRY MAIN SCARLET, slave owner, enters with a flourish. Right behind him is MADDOX, the HNIC.)*

ORRY MAIN: It's a beautiful day. A beautiful day to own slaves.

*(Everything freezes.)*

ANITA: At a time where America wrestles with its mortal soul.

*(Enter HARRY.)*

ANITA: One woman had the strength to stand up and pin down what was right.

*(Harry glides through the scene.)*

HARRY: *(Singing.)* I won't let you down/ So please don't give me up. *(She nods to each slave. Singing.)* Got have some faith in the sound./ It's the one good thing that I got.

*(They unfreeze and watch Harry exit, still singing.*

*Beat. They look each other. Beat. They look out. Beat. The slaves run off.*

*Orry Main and Overseer Jones unfreeze and see the slaves are gone.)*

ORRY MAIN: My nigras!?

*(They run off.)*

ANITA: In a very different America plans are underway to conquer the future by changing the past.

*(MIMI runs on.)*

MIMI: No!

*(JEREMY runs on. He holds a small mammy doll in his fist.)*

JEREMY: You have to do this!

MIMI: I won't!

*(Jeremy shoves the mammy doll into Mimi's hands.)*

JEREMY: In 1863 Harriet Tubman will lead Union Special Forces behind Confederate lines. And you are going to meet her there.

*(MUSIC - The relentless guitar crunch of heavy metal. I recommend I'm Gonna, by Pinky Tusadero's Whiteknuckle Ass Fuck.)*

ANITA: A man of science.

JEREMY: This is your chance to do what's right.

*(Mimi moves to exit. Orry Main and Overseer Jones enter blocking her escape.)*

ANITA: A thief.

MIMI: I won't.

*(Mimi moves towards the opposite exit. Harry and the Slaves enter blocking her escape.)*

ANITA: And the Moses of her people. On a collision course with history.

ORRY MAIN: I want my nigras back!

*(Orry Main and Overseer Jones reach out for the slaves and freeze.)*

ANITA: Riding a horse named danger.

*(The slaves huddle together and freeze.)*

ANITA: Down a street called destiny.

*(Mimi turns to Jeremy, who points to Harry and the slaves. He freezes.)*

ANITA: Carrying a banner of freedom.

*(Mimi turns back to Harry. Harry draws down on Mimi.)*

HARRY: What do you want?

MIMI: I'm here to help you start a war.

HARRY: I already got one, darlin.

*(Harry and Mimi freeze. A tableaux suggesting a movie poster. The wind blows. An awesome light effect happens. Maybe some smoke.)*

ANITA:  Harry and the Thief.

*(The tableaux breaks up and the actors exit and move into:)*

# WAR PANTIES. THINKING PANTIES.

*(Jeremy's big house. Mimi enters with two chairs.)*

ANITA: Fade in. Interior. Living room. A large craftsman's bungalow. Pasadena, California. Present day.

*(Mimi sits. Her clothes are disheveled and torn. There are blood stains. She puts her head is in her hands. Jeremy enters with two glasses of scotch.*

*Toast. Drink.)*

MIMI: Thanks, Jer for bailing me out. I'll get you cash-

JEREMY: No. No. No. We're family. Don't insult me.

MIMI: You saved my life.

JEREMY: Really?

MIMI: Pinky swear. I'm in a real tight place, man. I dunno. It's totally fucked up.

JEREMY: Are you crying?

MIMI: No. I just got profound shattering disappointment in my eyes.

JEREMY: Do you want to talk about it?

MIMI: No. What's up with you?

JEREMY: I'm glad you asked. I've built a time machine. *(Beat.)* My plan is to send someone back in time. 1863 exactly and deliver a cache of arms to Harriet Tubman. Would you like to join me on this quest?

MIMI: You're a fool. Seriously, what's going on with you?

JEREMY: I have built a time machine.

MIMI: Okay, I'll play along. And you are going to send some-one-

14

JEREMY: You.

MIMI: Okay. You are gonna send me back in time with guns for Harriet Tubman.

JEREMY: Yes.

MIMI: And what is Miz Tubman gonna do with said guns?

JEREMY: She will distribute them to black folks over the age of 14 both men and women. I am all for equality in the arm forces plus it increases your troop count. We will begin the insurrection in the south. Then move north. We will make Sherman's march look like a prance. I have a flexible and detailed battle plan. And once I am assured that transport is safe I will send back advisors and keep resupplying arms until it's done.

MIMI: Until what's done?

JEREMY: The overthrow of the United States government and the Establishment of a Free Black Republic with moi as Emperor.

MIMI: What about the other people?

JEREMY: What other people?

MIMI: You know.

JEREMY: Ah yes. White people. Yes. Them. I'm glad you've addressed this. Let's unpack it.

MIMI: Can't wait.

JEREMY: Well, I have a list. A list of options. Of solutions. I have a list and at the top is to crush them under the yoke of oppression. Actually, that is the only thing on the list.

MIMI: Okay. You want me to go back in time and give guns to Harriet Tubman to start a race war?

JEREMY: Race war?! God you make me sound like some chocolate covered Hitler. It is not a race war it is a war of equalization.

MIMI: Swapping black oppression for white oppression is not equalizing it is wrong.

JEREMY: Says the Oreo.

MIMI: I resent that.

JEREMY: And I resent you, madam. I resent that you would diminish the suffering of our people.

MIMI: I haven't even brought it up.

JEREMY: My point exactly. Your first question should have been: "Jeremy what have white people done to cause such rage?" But what comes out of your filthy pie hole? "Its wrong to hurt the white people." Sellout. You know, your criminal background should make you more in touch with our people?

MIMI: Dude, that is insulting on so many levels.

JEREMY: That's nothing compared with the insults our people have suffered. The many stings of hatred. The barbs of oppression-

MIMI: Dude, you have a PhD from Harvard.

JEREMY: The exception does not discount the rule.

MIMI: The president is black.

JEREMY: See previous answer. Plus addendum: A change in face doesn't fix a corrupt system.

MIMI: Uncle Carl is a cardiologist.

JEREMY: Do not bring my father into this. Never bring my father into any discussion. EVER!

MIMI: Sorry.

JEREMY: So are you in?

MIMI: No. Are you crazy?

JEREMY: Why not?

MIMI: Cuz. It's the stupidest-You can't travel back in time.

JEREMY: Raise your hand if you have a masters in Advance Mathematics. *(He raises his hand.)* Oh just me. Wait. Raise your hand if you have a PhD in Physics. *(He raises his hand.)* Me again.

MIMI: Raise your hand if you are a mad scientist.

JEREMY: Do this thing for me.

MIMI: Jer, please dude. Enough fun. I've had a shitty night.

JEREMY: You're for real? You're not going to do it?

MIMI: Read my face. Is there any indication that I have time for this stupid bullshit. *(Indicating her shirt.)* You know what this shit is here? That's blood vato. And some of it is even mine.

JEREMY: I'm sorry. I'm should have been more sensitive to your predicament. Sit. Let me get you another drink.

*(Jeremy exits. He returns with drinks.)*

JEREMY: Cheers.

MIMI: You weren't thinking of slipping me a Mickey and Shanghaiing me to the past?

*(Beat. Jeremy snatches the drink out of Mimi's hand. He sits. He sighs.)*

JEREMY: What happened? Maybe I can help. *(Sincerely.)* It will make you feel better.

MIMI: Promise.

JEREMY: Yes. Now tell me your story. *( To himself.)* So you can do what I want.

MIMI: My crew tried to kill me.

17

JEREMY: Really?

MIMI: Yes. We're doing a job. One minute I'm opening the safe. The next I'm being attacked. No provocation. I've know these guys for years. Why? Why would they do that?

JEREMY: I have no idea.

MIMI: Then I got fucking pinched. This was gonna be my last job. I was gonna buy land, leave the chaos of this life behind me, start clean, become new. Everything I've ever worked for. Just everything. Just gone.

JEREMY: I am sorry. I truly am. Everyone goes through something like this. So how do you want it?

MIMI: I don't want another drink.

JEREMY: Dr. Phil, Dr. Laura, Dr. Drew, The Mighty O. How shall I flavor your advise?

MIMI: I am way beyond advice.

JEREMY: Oh Zen. Excellent choice.

MIMI: You are going to do this anyway.

JEREMY: Please allow me to speak. Now you have probably heard this before but a classic is a classic for a reason. A man is walking through the forest and he comes across a tiger. With no provocation the tiger attacks the man. The man begins to run. The tiger begins to chase. The man runs over a cliff. He's lucky, he catches himself on a branch. So he's dangling hundreds of feet in the air, tiger above waiting for him and the man notices a strawberry plant growing out of a crack in the cliff.

*(Mimi opens her mouth to speak.)*

JEREMY: No questions. On the edge of the plant is the most reddest most perfect strawberry. The man plucks it, pops it into his mouth and it is the best tasting strawberry he's ever eaten. The end. Now, what have you learned from this story?

*(Beat. Mimi busts out laughing. It is a laughing crying hysteria mess.)*

MIMI: Oh my god I hate you so much right now.

JEREMY: The nugget of wisdom you should have gleaned, is that shit happens. It is how you handle your shit when the shit goes down that counts. Are you cool enough to enjoy the strawberry?

MIMI: What?

JEREMY: Everything is gone. What are you going to do about it?

MIMI: Am I cool enough to enjoy the strawberry?

JEREMY: I don't know. Are you?

MIMI: Am I cool enough to enjoy the strawberry?

JEREMY: Everything has crumbled. You just going to lie there?

MIMI: Am I cool enough to enjoy the strawberry?

JEREMY: Your life has been taken. Are you gonna take it back?

MIMI: Am I cool enough to enjoy the strawberry?

JEREMY: Tell it to me, girl.

MIMI: Am I cool enough to enjoy the strawberry.

JEREMY: Preach it! Preach it!

MIMI: Am I cool enough to enjoy the strawberry!

JEREMY: Tell it to Jesus now and all them folks in the back who don't believe.

MIMI: I am! I am! I am cool enough to enjoy the strawberry!

JEREMY: Hallelu!

MIMI: I am gonna kill all those motherfuckers!

JEREMY: Maybe you're not cool enough?

MIMI: No. I can enjoy the strawberry.

JEREMY: I don't think you can.

MIMI: I can. I can enjoy the fuck out of it.

JEREMY: No.

MIMI: You really don't think I can kill Ronnie, Bobby, Ricky and Mike?

JEREMY: Killing your crew is not the strawberry.

MIMI: Then who do I kill?

JEREMY: You are a magnificent creature. Violent. Ruthless. Cunning. A perfect storm of chaos. That's why I chose you. You're challenge is to channel all that energy towards good. That is your strawberry.

MIMI: That speech, the strawberry thing that was all about Harriet and the "time travel."

JEREMY: Yes. So have I convinced you to do it?

MIMI: No.

*(Mimi lunges at Jeremy and gets her hands around his throat.*

*There is a knock at the door.)*

JEREMY: Who is it?

RONNIE *(O.S.):* It's Ronnie.

BOBBY *(O.S.):* Bobby.

RICKY *(O.S):* Ricky.

20

MIKE *(O.S):* And Mike.

*(More knocking.)*

MIMI: Fuck they found me.

JEREMY: I called them.

MIMI: You what? Why!?

JEREMY: The adventure is-

*(More knocking.)*

JEREMY: Calling, Mimi. The job, your crew it is all part of the plan. There is no choice.

MIMI: I am the decider! I decide my fate. I am in control of this life.

*(Jeremy laughs an evil throaty laugh. Anita joins him. They stop.*

*More knocking.*

*Jeremy laughs an evil throaty laugh. Anita joins him. They stop.*

*More knocking.)*

RONNIE *(O.S.):* Cool it now with the knocking they know we're here.

BOBBY *(O.S.):* It's my prerogative. I can knock if I want to.

MIKE *(O.S.):* Hey Mimi, no use running.

BOBBY *(O.S.):* Every little step you take we will be there.

RICKY *(O.S.):* And we're gonna kill you.

MIMI: Come on fellas, we go back a long way, can't we work this out?

RICKY *(O.S.):* You shot me girl.

21

MIMI: You shot at me first.

MIKE *(O.S.):* Plus your cousin gave us a grip of loot.

MIMI: You back stabbing motherfuckers.

JEREMY: Never trust a big butt and a smile. Gentlemen thank you for making your presence known. I will call if you are needed. *(To Mimi.)* There is no escape. You will do this thing for me or bang bang your dead hole in your head.

MIMI: Motherfucker!

JEREMY: Yes. Established. So. Are. You. In?

MIMI: If this works after I get back from the past I am going to kill you. If it doesn't work, I am gonna kill you.

JEREMY: Girl, please, you say that after every family reunion. So, you're in.

MIMI: Yes.

*(As Jeremy and Mimi exit...*

*Anita enters. She is dressed in slave woman haute couture - Bright head wrap, skirt pinned up exposing red petticoat and thigh.)*

JEREMY: You're gonna do it?

MIMI: Fuck you.

ANITA: Destiny. Destiny. Destiny.

*(Mimi stops. Looks around. Is she hearing things?
Jeremy yanks her off stage.)*

# SWEET HARRY AND THE ROCK

*(The sounds of chains rattling, a whip on skin, bounce around for an uncomfortably long time. The sound cuts off.*

*Enter HARRY. She stands center.*

*Enter A WHITE MAN CARRYING A ROCK. He stands a few feet from Harry.)*

ANITA: When Harriet Tubman was 15 she put herself between her massa and a runaway slave.

*(White Man throws the rock at Harry hitting her in the head. She collapses. She gets up.*
*She tosses the rock back to White Man.)*

ANITA: When Harriet Tubman was 15 she put herself between her massa and a runaway slave.

*(White Man throws the rock at Harry hitting her in the head. She collapses. She gets up. She tosses the rock back to White Man.)*

ANITA: When Harriet Tubman was 15 she put herself between her massa and a runaway slave.

*(White Man throws the rock at Harry. She catches it. She stares at it in her hand. She stares at the White Man. He runs off.)*

ANITA: After that she was never the same.

*(Harry exits.)*

# SPECIAL PIES

*(Enter Shilo.)*

ANITA:  Cut to: Interior - Scarlet Plantation. Cook house. It has two big ole windows, that looks out over the yard. Shilo is inside cooking. The year 1858.

*(Set, cooking supplies, etc. should be suggested and pantomimed.*

*Shilo wears an apron.*

*Vivian enters. She has a bundle, it's a baby.)*

SHILO:  Good mornin', Vivian.

VIVIAN:  Hey.

SHILO:  Good mornin' little sweet baby. You pick a name out yet, for this little blue eyed angel?

VIVIAN:  I don't really wanna talk about it. *(Changing the subject.)* What you making?

SHILO:  Pies. It's a special day. *(Her voice gets low and ominous.)* Special pies. *(Her voice back to normal.)* And I'm making hoe cake sammies.

VIVIAN:  What's up with all the sandwiches?

SHILO:  They're not for me.

VIVIAN:  Who are they for?

SHILO:  Let me fix you one. They're delicious.

*(She goes into her description like a Antebellum Martha Steward. Finally an audience.)*

SHILO:  I cured the ham in salt, juniper berry and thyme. That goes on the hoe cake. Secret to my hoe cake. Besides love, is chopped corn and pinch of nutmeg. So ham on the hoe cake dressed with wild arugula and butter mixed with apricot preserves and mustard.

24

VIVIAN: Sounds yum. But no thanks. I am not here for break-fast. I have been meaning to stop by-

*(Vivian scopes the kitchen. She is looking for something.)*

SHILO: And visit with me!?

VIVIAN: Sorta.

SHILO: Oh goodie.

*(Vivian continues to snoop.)*

VIVIAN: What I need-

SHILO: I just love a good visit. And there's just not enough time in my day for visiting. I don't know why I am so busy? Well, of course I do. But it's best not to discuss un-pleasantness while visiting. You know the secret to my pie crust?

VIVIAN: *(Flatly.)* Besides love.

SHILO: Silly. Yes, love. And a little bit of hot pepper mixed with sugar. You have to grind it up real fine, till it's almost a powder. We must take pride in our work and enjoy what we do no matter the circumstance.

VIVIAN: Yeah. I guess.

*(Singing heard off.)*

HARRY *(O.S.):* I won't let you down/ So please don't give me up.

*(Shilo and Vivian go to the window.)*

SHILO: We must try to bare our indignities with grace.

HARRY *(O.S.):* Gotta have some faith in the sound/ It's the one good thing that I got./I won't let you down./So please don't give me up.

VIVIAN: I can think of a few alternatives.

25

HARRY *(O.S.)*: Cuz I really really love to stick around/Oh yeah.

*(Harry enters.)*

SHILO: *(To Harry.)* Good mornin'.

HARRY: Mornin.'

SHILO: Beautiful day.

HARRY: Indeed. Downright special.

*(Harry performs a gesture. It says "I'm here the freedom train is leaving get on board. Choo Choo." This gesture can broad or subtle.*

*Vivian and Shilo perform the gesture back to Harry. Then look at each other with surprise.)*

HARRY: Y'all have a pleasant day. And night.

*(Harry exits, singing.)*

HARRY: But today the way I play the game is not the same/ No way/Think I'm gonna get myself some happy.

VIVIAN: I need some of your special ingredients. I need someone quiet for a really long time. And I need them to go quickly.

SHILO: Yes, it's better that way. No mess. No noise. One minute they are complaining the soup has too much spice. And the meat isn't cooked all the way through and the potatoes got bugs in them or something. She says you are trying to ruin her dinner, make her look like a fool in front of her guest. Then she slaps you. In your own kitchen. Then her lip does that thing, when it curls and she makes threats about your station and your family. Then she makes good on those threats. So the next meal, you make it special. And then one minute she is complimenting your mince meat and then the next-silence. She went happy.

VIVIAN: What are you talking about?

SHILO: Oh, sorry. Nothing. Just tripped in a memory hole.

VIVIAN: Can you focus, please. I need it now, for tonight. And you have not seen me today.

*(Shilo pulls out a tiny satchel from her apron pocket and hands it to Vivian.)*

VIVIAN: How much do I use?

SHILO: For a subject 1-15 lbs, 1 pinch every 8 hours. Give them an hour or so of rest between doses. If you have a larger nuisance use the whole pouch.

VIVIAN: Won't that kill them?

SHILO: Good luck, dear.

*(Vivian backs away.)*

VIVIAN: Thanks, Shilo.

*(Vivian exits.*

*Shilo returns to her pies. She pulls another small satchel out of her pocket, it is identical to Vivian's. She opens it and sprinkles it liberally on her pies.)*

# HER GOT TWO DRESSES

*(Maddox and Orry Main enter.)*

ANITA: Establishing shot. Exterior Scarlet Plantation, porch. Maddox and Orry Main stand looking out.

*(Anita exits.)*

ORRY MAIN: We have a big day today. We must prepare for Mr. Preston Dillard's arrival tomorrow. We're gonna have a sale. Here's the list. Mrs. Scarlet has her heart set on new bedroom furniture and a new carriage. So I have to raise some funds.

MADDOX: I shall go over the books, sir. I am sure we can find the extra money.

ORRY MAIN: You should look at the list.

MADDOX: My name is on the list, isn't it.

ORRY MAIN: Yeah.

MADDOX: You're selling me.

ORRY MAIN: I know.

MADDOX: Who is going to manage the work schedules for the field and house workers? Who is going to see to it that the bills are paid and that the books are balanced? Who is going to manage your correspondence? Help Miss Scarlet plan parties? Order farm tools? Pick out your clothes in the morning?

ORRY MAIN: I guess I will.

*(Maddox laughs.)*

ORRY MAIN: Don't you dare laugh at me. Just like the other plantation owners at our monthly card game. They said I'd soon as sell Mrs. Scarlet than get rid of you.

28

MADDOX: Is her name on the list?

ORRY MAIN: Don't take it personally, Maddox. I adore you. But this is business. And don't look so glum. I'm sure you will find a wonderful new owner and I hear Mississippi is beautiful this time of year.

MADDOX: Shall we go over the list, sir and calculate your prospective ill gotten gains. There is Miss Shilo the cook-

ORRY MAIN: They never did find out what happen to her pervious owner.

MADDOX: She sold Shilo's family and then she died. 1,500 dollars for Miss Shilo. Knox, stable hand 1,300 dollars. Vivian and child-

ORRY MAIN: Oh this is so unpleasant. Let's just stand here a moment. Me and you, together, for the last time. *(Beat.)* It's a beautiful day. *(Beat.)* A beautiful day to own slaves. *(Beat.)* To plan the sale of slaves. Look at them out there on my land. Skin dark as the rich earth, soft as cotton. Do you hear their songs? The dark majestic soulfulness of their voices. It touches me so.

MADDOX: Obviously, you are a man of deep and tender feelings.

ORRY MAIN: My boy, you understand me like no one else. My handsome boy. What am I gonna do without your wisdom?

MADDOX: I imagine you will buy another who looks just like me?

ORRY MAIN: You are droll. You are charming. Simply charming.

MADDOX: Well appreciation is always a gift no matter the sender. Thank you, sir.

ORRY MAIN: I just like being around you so much.

MADDOX: There is the option of forgoing the sale.

ORRY MAIN: No. But, I'd like to give you a hug.

MADDOX: Your verbal praise is sufficient.

ORRY MAIN: *(Opening his arms. Advancing.)* Nope. I'm coming in.

*(Orry embraces Maddox. Harry enters.)*

MADDOX: *(Seeing Harriet.)* Oh Thank God.

ORRY MAIN: *(Placing his head on Maddox's shoulder.)* I know it feels like home, don't it?

*(She and Maddox give each other the Freedom Train signal.*

*Orry releases Maddox. He sees Harry.)*

ORRY MAIN: Aint she something?

MADDOX: Isn't she.

ORRY MAIN: Majestic. Commanding. Do I own her?

MADDOX: No. You do not own her. She is on loan from Senator Calhoun. Her name is Gretchen. She is a laundress and a mute.

ORRY MAIN: *(Waving to Harry.)* Morning.

HARRY: How's it going?

MADDOX: Splendid. I just told him you were a mute.

ORRY MAIN: She can talk!

MADDOX: Very good, sir. I hope we all share your lighting quick wit.

HARRY: Honey, I'm legendary. *(To Orry Main.)* Good morning, sir. My name is Minty.

ORRY MAIN: You got her name wrong too! Oh Maddox you are making me regret my regret in selling you.

HARRY: I would like to extend apologies for the absents of Gretchen. She has taken ill. And I will be filling in for her. Y'all have a lovely day.

ORRY MAIN: Gal! Come back here. I didn't dismiss you. I don't know how they run things over there at 12 Oaks but here one is dismissed. There's something about you. How many dresses they give you at the Oaks?

HARRY: Two.

ORRY MAIN: Bit high on the hog. But I understand. You're valuable. And value has to be rewarded. My Maddox, he's got four pair of pants.

*(Maddox holds up four fingers.)*

ORRY MAIN: Look here, I am in the middle of some personnel changes. If you are interested leading a different life. Note I said different not better. 12 Oaks seems to take good care of you. You got two dresses.

*(Orry launches into a Price is Right like pitch. Harry jumps up and down, squealing like a game show contestant.*

*Maddox watches, all the dignity draining from his face.)*

ORRY MAIN: But not a Planation within 10 miles can top the amenities we have. How'd you like a cabin with a solid wood door. Just a hop, skip and a jump from your cozy corn husk mattress to work. From our famous fall corn shucking to our generous Christmas bonus. Last year me and the misses gave out peppermint candies to the pickinnies and ribbons to women. You like ribbons, gal?

HARRY: Ribbons! Ribbons!

ORRY MAIN: Yes, folks are happy here at the Scarlet Plantation. It's a great place to be.

*(Things go back to normal.)*

ORRY MAIN: Aint that right, Maddox.

MADDOX: Yes, as the days wear on, my self loathing and rage grows exponentially.

ORRY MAIN: See. Happy.

HARRY: Sir, you flatter me.

ORRY MAIN: Of course I do. I'll talk to Calhoun about getting you out here permanently. You're dismissed.

HARRY: Good day to you, Mr. Scarlet, sir. Mr. Maddox till we meet again.

MADDOX: I shall count the hours.

*(Harry exits.)*

ORRY MAIN: You think my pitch was too aggressive?

*(As Maddox and Orry Main exit.)*

MADDOX: Shall we proceed with our tasks. I have things to accomplish before my impending departure.

ORRY MAIN: It makes me sad to think on it. Let's pretend that it's not going to happen.

MADDOX: Pretend till your heart's content, sir.

# YOU'RE NOT GOING & WE'RE NOT DATING

*(Knox enters he crosses the space. Harry enters and falls in behind him.*
*Harry mimics Knox's movements. She hums (Freedom.) Knox stops. He turns. Harry turns. He turns back. So does Harry. He moves forward with Harry following.*
*The action repeats. On the 3rd time, Harry stands still as Knox turns. He jumps.*
*Harry gives Knox the signal. Knox returns it.)*

KNOX: *(Looking her over.)* You're Harriet Tubman? You're very short.

HARRY: You're very perceptive.

KNOX: Yes, I know.

HARRY: Listen for my song, then assemble at the north side of the barn.

*(Vivian enters. She has a bundle it's a baby.)*

VIVIAN: General Tubman, I just wanted to formally introduce myself. I'm Vivian and it's an honor, ma'am, just an honor.

HARRY: Yeah. Nice to-

KNOX: Wait. Naw. No way. You aint going.

VIVIAN: You don't own me.

KNOX: It's too dangerous. You're just a girl. And you got a baby, it's gonna make noise.

VIVIAN: You don't need to worry about that. And the General ferries women all the time.

HARRY: I don't discriminate when it comes to freedom. All are wel-

KNOX: I'm putting my foot down. This what you're gonna do. You'll hire yourself out, save some money and buy freedom for little what's his name. Vicarious freedom is better than none at all.

33

VIVIAN: Then, why don't you stay and raise what's his name?

KNOX: No. I am going out west. I am gonna be a vaquero. That's Spanish for cowboy.

VIVIAN: Bully for you.

*(Knox gives Harry a look then pulls Vivian aside. Harriet Tubman sighs, exasperated.)*

KNOX: What do we really know about this Tubman? She might be mad. She might abandon us in woods. She could turn us in or worse. But I am a man. If she goes all girly I can always use my wits to get to freedom. But I can't do that if I have to look after you and what's his name. Viv, I don't wanna leave you behind but one of us has got to get free. For mama. We gotta do it for mama!

VIVIAN: Mama's dead. I'm not staying here one more night. And you aint gonna stop me.

KNOX: Vivian. I put my foot down.

VIVIAN: My foot down.

KNOX: Now you are gonna stop all this foolishness

VIVIAN: Stop all this foolishness.

KNOX: Vivian.

VIVIAN: -Vian.

KNOX: I'm serious.

VIVIAN: -serious.

KNOX: Stop that right-

VIVIAN: Stop that-

*(Harry exits as Overseer Jones enter. Vivian and Knox are too busy fighting to notice.)*

KNOX: Listen-

VIVIAN: Listen-

JONES: What you gotta tell me darlin? *(To Knox.)* Boy, Mr. Scarlet wants his horse. *(To Vivian.)* Morin' Vivian. Sleep well last night?

VIVIAN: No.

*(Jones rubs Vivian's back.)*

JONES: Baby keep you up?

*(Vivian walks away.)*

VIVIAN: Gross.

JONES: Vivian, you're not allowed to walk away from me.

*(Vivian doesn't move.)*

JONES: Come here.

*(Vivian doesn't move. Knox moves to Jones' side.)*

JONES: I thought I told you to get that horse boy?

KNOX: Ah don't be like that, Jonesy. I wanna stay and see how this plays out.

JONES: Vivian, come here. Don't make me come over there, gal.

*(Jones marches over to Vivian.)*

JONES: I swear to God, Vivian.

*(Vivian turns. Serving up Gossip Girl, Melrose, Dynasty. Drama.)*

VIVIAN: I'm not afraid of you anymore.

JONES: *(Tenderly.)* Baby girl, what happened? I am sensing tension in our relationship.

VIVIAN: Omigawd. You are so stupid. We are not dating, Maynard.

JONES: *(Wounded.)* Dating?! I never said we-Of course were not- I'm a- and you're a- It just aint fittin.' Dating!?

VIVIAN: This is what I'm talking about.

JONES: What?

VIVIAN: Why are you hurt? You don't get to be hurt.

JONES: I aint. But why you gotta be all like *(Mocking.)* "We aint dating." I know we got off to a rocky start but-

VIVIAN: You delusional motherfucker! Why can't you be like other overseers? Just show up at night do your thing and don't say boo after. Maybe cop a feel while I am hanging the sheets, but give me my days.

JONES: But I enjoy being around you.

VIVIAN: *(To Knox.)* Do you believe this guy over here?

JONES: We got a baby now.

VIVIAN: Yeah? And? So?

JONES: He's so beautiful. We made him. Look at our boy. That's glory, girl.

*(Vivian exits. Knox applauds.)*

KNOX: Damn, now that's drama.

*(Jones get in Knox's face. During the following exchange they posture, puffing their chest, flex.)*

KNOX: Jonesy, I'm gonna kill you for what you did to my sister. Might not be now but best believe it's coming.

JONES: Go get that horse, boy.

KNOX:  Yes, sir, boss, sir.

*(Singing heard off.)*

HARRY *(O.S.)*:  All we have to now/Is take these lies and make them true somehow.

*(Jones exits towards the sound. Knox exits the opposite direction.*

*Harry enters from the opposite side of the space, crosses and exits.)*

HARRY:  All we have see is that I don't belong to you/ And you don't belong to me/Yeah Yeah.

# HOW TIME TWERKS

*(Anita enters. She is dressed in a 40's style travel suit. She has a small valise.)*

ANITA: Jump cut to the present. Interior. Jeremy's big house.

*(Enter Mimi.*

*She is dressed for the past in a simple long skirt and cotton blouse. She stuffs a map in her pocket.*

*She stands center.)*

ANITA: You all up in the face of history, now how you gonna act?

*(With big stylized gestures. Mimi covers her ears. Mimi cover her eyes. Mimi covers her mouth.*

*She repeats the gestures, they get fast frenzied.)*

ANITA: Freeze Frame. Reverse.

*(Mimi freezes. Mimi reverses her actions.*

*She enters again stands center.)*

ANITA: You all up in the face of history, now how you gonna act?

*(Mimi does the Running Man in slow motion.*

*She moves faster and faster and faster and faster.)*

ANITA: History is a heavy thing. Far from your control. Born into it. There is no escape. The laws of physics say there is no difference between the past and the future. They are with you in the bed of the present. All y'all spooned together under a blanket of collective wounds. Who farted?

*(Mimi collapses.)*

ANITA: You all up in the face of history.

*(Anita removes a gun (Sig P two-twenty-two) from her valise and sits it next to Mimi.)*

ANITA: Now. How you gonna act? Twerk!

*(Mimi twerks.*

*Mimi sees the gun. She stops. She picks up the gun. Checks the clip then slams it back in the gun. She chambers a round. She aims at the audience. How you like me now?*

*Mimi twerks with the gun in her hand.*

*Anita looks at her. Smiles.*

*Anita closes her valise and exits.*

*Mimi continues twerking.*

*Jeremy enters.)*

JEREMY: Why you twerkin?

*(Mimi stops.)*

JEREMY: Playing crazy aint gonna get you outta this.

*(He pulls a small "Mammy" doll from his pocket and hands it to Mimi.)*

JEREMY: This is your transport device. Under Mammy's skirt are three buttons. Red is for the past green is for the present and yellow is --

MIMI: The future.

JEREMY: A flashlight.

MIMI: What happens when I press the button? Is it like Terminator? Am I gonna show up somewhere naked? Or is like 12 Monkeys? You got some big plastic tube hidden around here?

JEREMY: No tube.

MIMI: You built a ship/car thing like Time Cop?

JEREMY: No ship. Just push the red button.

MIMI: Then what?

JEREMY: You end up in the past.

MIMI: How?

JEREMY: Theoretically you get broken down and put back together.

MIMI: Theoretically? With all my parts put back in the right places?

JEREMY: Shit I hope.

MIMI: And not naked.

JEREMY: Shit I hope not.

MIMI: Just push the red button?

JEREMY: Yes. Now would be good. We aint got all the time in the world. *(He laughs at his own joke.)*

MIMI: Just push the red button.

*(Mimi takes a deep breath.)*

MIMI: This is so stupid...

*(Another a deep breath.*

*She goes to push the button.)*

JEREMY: Wait! Not here. In the other room.

MIMI: Why?

*(Jeremy just looks at her.*

40

*Mimi exits.)*

JEREMY: *(Calling off.)* See the tarp?

MIMI *(O.S.)*: Yeah.

JEREMY: Stand in the center where all the towels are.

MIMI *(O.S.)*: Why?

JEREMY: Just do it!

MIMI: Fine. I'm on the towels. Jer?

JEREMY: Yeah.

MIMI *(O.S.)*: Now what?

JEREMY: Push the red button, bitch.

MIMI *(O.S.)*: Okay I'm pushing the red-

*(The sound of time moving backwards.)*

JEREMY: Mimi. Mimi?

*(Jeremy runs off. Pause then the sound of clapping and self congratulations.)*

# BODICE SAVED IS A BODICE EARNED

ANITA:  In the 18th and 19th century, 20 million people were enslaved. The American way of life depended on slavery.

*(Enter Jones. He waves a little American flag on a stick.*

*Enter Vivian from the opposite side of the space.)*

ANITA:  Slaves owned nothing.

*(They cross towards each other.)*

ANITA:  Not even themselves.

*(Vivian and Jones meet in the center.*

*Vivian goes one way. Jones steps in front of her. She goes the opposite way. He does the same.*

*This happens again. Then they stand face to face.)*

ANITA:  Most slave had only one outfit to wear-one dress or one pair of pants and a shirt.

*(Jones rips Vivian's bodice.*

*Pause. Vivian repairs her shirt. (Yay Velcro!)*

*They back up.)*

ANITA:  Slaves owned nothing.

*(They cross towards each other.)*

ANITA:  Not even themselves.

*(Vivian and Jones meet in the center.*

*Vivian goes one way. Jones steps in front of her. She goes the opposite way. He does the same.*

*This happens again. Then they stand face to face.)*

ANITA: Most slave had only one outfit to wear-one dress or one pair of pants and a shirt.

*(Jones rips Vivian's bodice.*

*Pause. Vivian repairs her shirt. (Yay Velcro!)*

*They back up.)*

ANITA: Slaves owned nothing.

*(They cross towards each other.)*

ANITA: Not even themselves.

*(Vivian breaks out running. Jones tries to block her. She punk fakes and spins off his body, like a football player and exits.*

*Jones runs after her.)*

ANITA: Under such conditions it was inevitable that some slaves escaped.

# LOOKS LIKE THE ROAD TO HEAVEN

*(Orry is passed out in a chair, an empty pie tin on the floor next to him.*

*Shilo is in his lap with her apron wrapped around his throat.*

*She is choking him.)*

ANITA: Interior. Dinning room Scarlet Plantation.

HARRY *(O.S.)*: *(Singing.)* Freedom/Freedom/Freedom/You got to give for what you take.

*(Maddox enters, he has a violin case.)*

SHILO: Maddox! You're going too? Yippee!!!

MADDOX: Madam please lower your voice.

SHILO: *(Quietly.)* Yippee!

MADDOX: And remove yourself from that man.

SHILO: But he's not dead yet.

MADDOX: Good effort. Give me your hand. We do not have time for this.

*(Maddox helps Shilo off Orry.)*

SHILO: I don't understand. He ate a whole pie.

*(They exit.*

*Enter Jones and Vivian.*

*Jones lays on the floor. He's passed out. The bundle lays next to him. It's a baby.*

*Vivian stands over Jones, she has a chair raised over her head.)*

ANITA: Cut away shot: Vivian and Knox's slave cabin.

*(Anita exits. Knox enters.)*

KNOX: Vivian!

44

VIVIAN: I'm gonna kill him. Almost finished.

*(Vivian pulls back for a swing. Knox takes the chair from her. He pulls back for a swing. Noises off. Vivian stops him.)*

VIVIAN: What's that? Get down.

*(They crouch.*

*Knox creeps to the window and peeks out.)*

HARRY *(O.S.)*: (Singing.) Freedom/ Oh Freedom/My Freedom/ You got to give for what you take/Freedom/Hold on to my Freedom

KNOX: I gotta go.

VIVIAN: We gotta go.

KNOX: No.

VIVIAN: What you think gonna happen to me when he wakes up?

KNOX: Goddamn it Vivian. Okay you can go.

VIVIAN: I wasn't asking permission.

*(Vivian starts to creep off.)*

KNOX: Wait. Don't forget what's his name.

VIVIAN: Fuck that white baby.

*(Vivian exits.*

*Knox moves towards the bundle. Knox stops. He looks at the bundle.)*

HARRY *(O.S.)*: *(Singing.)* My Freedom/You got to give for what you take/Yeah/You got to give for what you/Give for what you/Give for what you/ Give/ May not be what you want from me/But this is the way it's got to be.

*(Knox exits.)*

# BAND ON THE RUN

*(The sound of time moving backwards.*

*Anita enters with her valise.)*

ANITA: Smash cut into the Maryland woods. Night. 1858. A bright unearthly light flashes illuminating the foliage.

*(A thud. Then retching. This goes on for a while.*

*Mimi stumbles into the space.*

*She checks herself making sure all her parts are in place.)*

MIMI: Fuck me.

ANITA: Destiny. Destiny. Destiny.

*(She hears something. Away goes the map out comes the gun. She creeps off.*

*Anita sees something off in the distance.)*

ANITA: Taxi!

*(Anita scampers off.*

*Harry and the Band of Slaves enter.*

*They creep through the space, moving through imaginary streams, flattening themselves against imaginary trees, crawling through bushes.*

*A noise. The Band freezes.*

*Harry gathers them in a huddle. She puts her fingers to her lips, shhhh! She exits.)*

KNOX: Y'all see that freaky light?

SHILO: Oh Lawd we are caught for sure.

MADDOX: Do not worry, Miss Shilo. I imagine that Master Scarlet and his machinations will make quite a deal more noise. I am sure it is but a lonely traveler.

KNOX: You got to wonder about a conductor who would walk us right up on someone. Someone with a freaky light.

*(Vivian moves around stomping her feet.)*

SHILO: *(Indicating Vivian.)* I think we should stay put.

VIVIAN: I'm just so totally cold. I forgot my jacket.

KNOX: You also forgot your baby.

VIVIAN: I don't want to talk about it.

KNOX: How could you leave what's his name?

VIVIAN: You were the last on to see him. Why didn't you take him? You are just as guilty as I am.

KNOX: I am not.

VIVIAN: You are too.

KNOX: Am not.

VIVIAN: Are too.

KNOX: Am not.

*(Harry enters. She throws her head back. This is not happening. She takes a deep cleansing breath and approaches Vivian and Knox.)*

VIVIAN: Are to.

KNOX: Am not.

VIVIAN: Are too.

KNOX: Am not infin-

HARRY: Excuse me. I don't mean to interrupt. You through? Great. Can we not have the talking? Especially when we are sneaking around the woods. There's no talking when we're doing that. Actually there is no talking ever. Sorry if that wasn't clear. Everyone understand? Please nod if you understand.

SHILO: Have they found us?

KNOX: We have to go back.

HARRY: Okay you don't understand. That what you just did that was talking. Don't do that anymore. No one found us. It was just a lonely traveler.

KNOX: General, my sister left her baby.

HARRY: *(To Vivian.)* On purpose or accidentally?

VIVIAN: On purpose.

HARRY: We're moving out.

KNOX: I didn't listen to my instincts I should have killed Jones when I had the chance.

HARRY: No more talking.

KNOX: I should have taken what's his name. I have to make this right. We're going back for what's his name. Then we're going after Jones.

HARRY: You don't know what this is, do you? This is about me. Me. Saving you. See this is my world. A few of the things I control in my world are: the nature of time and space and you. You are not free here. When I get you to the other side, your life is your own. Until then do as I say shut the fuck up and welcome to the adventure.

KNOX: I'm putting my foot down.

HARRY: Well, I guess it's decided then.

*(She draws down on Knox.)*

HARRY: In a few seconds you are going to stop talking and we're gonna move out. Now you get to decide how that's gonna happen. Choose wisely, son.

*(Beat. Knox runs.)*

48

HARRY: Shit.

*(Everyone looks at Harry.)*

VIVIAN: I got him.

*(Vivian takes off after Knox.)*

HARRY: Shit. *(To Maddox and Shilo.)* Wait here.

*(Harry takes off.*

*Shilo and Maddox look around and at each other with unease, they creep back into the darkness.)*

# HERE WITHOUT YOU

*(Anita enters.)*

ANITA: High top fade. Exterior Scarlet Plantation, early the next morning.

*(Orry stumbles into the space carrying a pie tin with an apron wrapped around his neck.)*

ORRY MAIN: Maddox?! Maddox?!

*(Jones enters. He carries a bundle. It's a baby.)*

JONES: Sir, are you wounded?

ORRY MAIN: Yes. My Maddox is gone.

JONES: Sir, Vivian and Knox are also gone.

*(Orry swoons. Jones tries to catch him but he's got that bundle. It's a baby.*

*Orry crumples to the ground. He begins weeping softly.)*

JONES: Sir, please don't, it's going to be alright.

ORRY MAIN: Maddox was my best friend. I was gonna to sell him. Thousands of dollars. My Maddox. Gone! And with the others that's....10 grand!

*(He weeps harder.)*

JONES: Come on, sir no more of that.

*(Orry is inconsolable.)*

ORRY MAIN: 10 grand! My Maddox! How will I breath?

JONES: You need a drink, sir. (Calling off.) Shilo! Shilo! Shilo! Shilo?

*(Jones rushes off. He returns a moment later.)*

50

JONES: She's gone.

ORRY MAIN: How shall I eat?

*(He begins to cry again.)*

ORRY MAIN: I want my nigras back!

JONES: Come on get up.

ORRY MAIN: My nigras! My nigras, my nigras, my nigras!

JONES: Goddamn it, sir, act like a man. We are gonna get them back. They belong to us. This is their home. We love them. They got no right to leave us. We have to get them back. Get them back and show them how much we value them. Get them back and show them how much we need them. Get them back and show them we can't get along without them. *(Aside with intensity.)* Make them love us. This is what we do.

ORRY MAIN: What do we do?

JONES: Set the dogs on them and ride them down.

ORRY MAIN: With torches?

JONES: Yeah, that'll scare them good.

ORRY MAIN: Good plan.

JONES: Dogs first, sir?

*(Orry stops and stares sharply into the distance.)*

JONES: Mister Scarlet? Sir, you're not gonna start crying again, are ya?

ORRY MAIN: No, Jones, I am over that. Now I am vexed. I am going to kill him. I am going to tell my Maddox that I love him then I am going to blow a hole in his chest.

JONES: What about the rest of them?

ORRY MAIN: I will kill them as well.

JONES: Even Vivian?

ORRY MAIN: All. When I find them I am going to kill them all.

JONES: Sir, that's a lot of money to just–

ORRY MAIN: We'll split up at Dawson's Creek. You take the high road. I'll take the low road. Then we'll swoop around and catch 'em in the middle.

JONES: *(Reeling at the idea.)* What if I find them first?

ORRY MAIN: Excellent question. *(Thinking.)* Wound them. Knee cap, Achilles tendon, gut shot. Just keep them alive till I arrive. Three shots in the air and I will come running. Let's go they can't have gotten far. *(Noticing the bundle.)* What's that?

JONES: This is Malik, my son.

ORRY MAIN: Jonesy, you are so white trash, son. You aren't suppose to claim them. Come on let's go get the hounds.

*(Orry exits.)*

ANITA: Close up. Jones' sad face. A single tear falls.

*(Jones exits.)*

ANITA: Match cut: a sliver of dying moonlight hits the ground. We are back in the woods.

*(Anita exits.)*

# BAND ON THE RUN II: THE TRIP UP

*(Shilo and Maddox enter.*

*They sit. Maddox takes Shilo's arm, closes his eyes and begins to play her arm as if it were a violin. - I suggest Beethoven's Symphony #6- Upon Waking in the Country.*
*The music swells around them. They lose themselves inside of it. The sound overtakes the space.*

*Mimi crosses the space. She doesn't see Maddox and Shilo. They don't see her.*

*The music swells as Maddox finishes with a flourish. He releases Shilo's arm.*

*They sit in silence for a moment.)*

SHILO:  That was the most beautiful thing I have ever heard.

MADDOX:  Miss Shilo.

SHILO:  Yes, Mr. Maddox.

MADDOX:  I would like you promise me something. Promise me that you will do whatever it takes to get to Paris.

SHILO:  Oh. Mr. Maddox. I will never reach Paris. It was foolish of me to have spoken about it.

MADDOX:  Miss Shilo. You are the down trodden and weary that ballads are written for. You are the forever Quixotic hero of legends. You are hope and perseverance personified. It is your destiny to succeed.

SHILO:  Oh my God, you totally like me.

MADDOX:  Promise me you will fulfill your destiny.

SHILO:  What about your destiny, Mr. Maddox?

MADDOX:  I am pursuing it as we speak.

SHILO:  Oh. Mr. Maddox.

*(They look deeply at one and other.*

*Lights go full.*

*Harry enters. Behind her Vivian who is leading, Knox, who is bounded and gagged.*

*Harry begins to look around.)*

VIVIAN: Fuckin' A. That was awesome! Ohhh the woods at dawn! I never dreamed, chasing someone down could feel this good. Man when you got them niggas in your sights and they're giving it everything they got - you're a fast runner little brother - and you take them down anyway. Yeah! Yeah! Fuck yeah! *(Noticing Harry.)* I'm talking loud, huh?

HARRY: Yes.

VIVIAN: And it's daytime, right?

HARRY: Yes.

VIVIAN: That's not good, right?

HARRY: Yes.

VIVIAN: My bad.

HARRY: Listen up. This is gonna hafta do for today. *(To Shilo and Maddox.)* Excuse me, you two. I'm speaking. We camp here. It's not too bad. *(Indicating in front of the band.)* We've go excellent visual coverage with this thick stand of bushes, and the brook should take care of any noise. But let's keep communication to essentials only. Into the bushes. Move. Move.

*(The band moves up out of the playing space into some "bushes.")*

HARRY: Break out chow.

*(During the scene Harry checks the perimeter, sets booby traps etc.)*

SHILO: Mr. Maddox?

MADDOX: Miss Shilo?

SHILO: Would you like a sandwich?

MADDOX: Thank you.

SHILO: Excuse me, General, would you like a sandwich? It's spice cured ham on a hoe cake, dressed with wild arugula and apricot mustard preserves.

HARRY: I don't eat on mission.

SHILO: Vivian. Did y'all bring food?

VIVIAN: No.

SHILO: Lucky I'm here. Take a sandwich, dear.

VIVIAN: Thanks.

*(Shilo offers one to Knox.)*

SHILO: Excuse me, General, may I untie Knox so he can enjoy one of my tasty sandwiches?

HARRY: Sure. I figured he's learned his lesson.

VIVIAN: Can we keep the gag in?

*(Shilo unties Knox, removes his gag and gives him a sandwich.)*

KNOX: I was only trying-

HARRY: To be a hero. Don't. There's only one hero on this journey, son. And she's wearing a bandana.

VIVIAN: I'm wearing a bandana. So is Shilo.

SHILO: That's true. I am wearing a bandana.

HARRY: I'm the hero. Me. *(To Vivian.)* You know you didn't have to leave your kid.

VIVIAN: I didn't want it. He's got blue eyes, know what I'm saying.

HARRY: Yeah. That sorta thing goes on lot. Sorry. Listen up everyone-get some sleep we have along walk a head of us. I got the watch.

*(Everyone settles down.*

*Harry gets in position for the watch. She has a fit of narcolepsy. She blacks out.*

*The band rises and stands over her.)*

MADDOX: Dear God.

SHILO: General?

VIVIAN: Holy shit.

KNOX: I feel strangely vindicated.

*(Mimi enter, consulting her map.)*

VIVIAN: Shhh.

KNOX: *(Mocking her.)* Shhh.

MADDOX: Quiet. Someone is out there.

*(Knox pokes his head out of the bushes.*

*Harry's eyes pop open.*

*Mimi turns. Knox pokes his head back in.)*

MIMI: Where is everyone?

KNOX: It's a sistah.

SHILO: Do we know her?

*(Knox pokes his head out.)*

MIMI: Where's the war?

*(Knox begins to crawl out.*

*Harry springs awake. She grabs Knox and pulls him back in.*

*Mimi exits.)*

SHILO: Excuse me General, I don't mean to disturb you. But you passed out.

HARRY: It's nothing. I'm fine.

MADDOX: Are you sure you are alright, ma'am?

KNOX: No. She aint alright.

HARRY: I'm fine.

KNOX: You aint.

HARRY: You wanna another dance with me, son?

SHILO: General, are you sure-

HARRY: I am fine! And I am completely aware of what's going on when it happens.

MADDOX: This is a reoccurring trouble?

SHILO: You means this happens all the time?

VIVIAN: What's your damage?

KNOX: We're doomed.

HARRY: Everyone shut up! People walk through the woods, there's nothing strange about that. We were not detected. Everything is fine. Now go back to sleep and let me do my job. That's an order. Sleep.

*(The band reluctantly settles back down.*

*The tension begins to ease and they drift off to sleep.*

*Moments later Harry passes out.)*

# THESE ARE NOT THE DROIDS
## YOU ARE LOOKING FOR

*(Mimi enters.*

*She is consulting the map. She realizes it is upside down. She rights it and continues on.*

*Anita enters. She is wearing a Safari outfit (Streep "Out of Africa" inspired?) or maybe a Boy Scout outfit? Sexy hiker? Whatever the choice, her ensemble says: I'm ready for a jaunt in the great outdoors.*

*Anita crosses the space looking around then exits.*

*Jones enters-obviously he doesn't see the band of runaways "hidden" behind the "bushes."*

*Jones has a shot gun with a belt of buckshot slung across his chest. He also has a bundle strapped to his back, like a Yoroba woman working in the field or a hipster mom shopping for vegetables in the Mission District. It's a baby.)*

JONES: That's a lot of knee caps I gotta shoot, Malik. Don't tell no one, but Daddy don't think he can blow off Mommy's knees.

*(Mimi enters.*

*Harry bolts awake.*

*The Band remains asleep.)*

JONES: Hey gal, come here.

*(Mimi looks up at Jones then back to her map.)*

JONES: Gal, I am taking to you. Come here.

*(Mimi does not look up or move.)*

JONES: Don't make me come over there, gal.

*(Mimi walks over to Jones.)*

MIMI: Hey is this South Carolina?

JONES: I am the one asking the questions. You see buncha niggers round here?

MIMI: That like a murder of crows?

JONES: You aint from around here is you? You contraband?

*(Jones trains is gun on Mimi, who takes it from him effortlessly. Jones instinctively reaches for the bundle on his back.)*

MIMI: I am gonna ask you again, is this South Carolina?

JONES: This here's Maryland.

MIMI: Where's the war?

JONES: What war?

MIMI: What year is it?

JONES: How come you don't know the year?

MIMI: Cuz Ies just a dumb nigger wandering the forest primeval.

JONES: What's primeval? Oh Lawdy lawdy! Youes a Hoodoo Voodoo woman. Save me Baby Jesus! Oh Lawd. Youes a demon come to fetch me to Hades for my sins. If you are such a one I ask that you spare my boy.

MIMI: Yeah, I am a Hoodoo Voodoo demon woman and I need to know the year.

JONES: 1858.

MIMI: Seriously!? Damn it Jeremy! That "buncha niggers" you're looking for you got any idea which way they are headed.

JONES: I expect north.

MIMI: Don't be smart ass. Which way is north?

*(Jones points.)*

MIMI: *(Handing his gun back.)* Go home, mister. Seek and sin no more.

*(Vivian pops her head out. Harry puts her finger to her lips--shhhh.)*

JONES: No, ma'am I have to find them and warn them. Master Scarlet is looking for them and he's fixin to kill them all. I gotta protect my baby's mama.

MIMI: Don't let me stop you.

JONES: Thank you for not taking me to hell.

MIMI: I'm sure you'll get there eventually.

JONES: Excuse me, Miss Hoodoo, maybe we can travel together? You aint from here. I can help you.

MIMI: I work alone.

*(Jones doesn't move. He watches Mimi.*

*Mimi takes out the mammy doll. She examines it.)*

MIMI: I'm three years off. Or is it four?

*(She stuffs the doll in her bosom, its head peeks out over her cleavage.)*

MIMI: How the fuck am I suppose to find Tubman now? Damn you Jeremy!

JONES: Bye.

*(Mimi exits.)*

VIVIAN: General, we gonna leave?

HARRY: No.

VIVIAN: Should I wake the others?

HARRY:  No.

VIVIAN:  You know that woman looking for you?

HARRY:  No.

VIVIAN:  You think she's a demon?

HARRY:  No.

VIVIAN:  What are we gonna do?

HARRY:  Stop asking questions. Wait until dark and be quiet.

VIVIAN:  I can do that. *(Beat.)* You aint gonna pass out again?

*(Mimi enters.)*

MIMI:  This looks famili-

JONES:  Howdy.

| MIMI: Goddamn it! I'm walking in circles. | JONES: You're walking in circles. |
|---|---|

*(Mimi stops and looks at Jones. She begins to exit. She stops.)*

MIMI:  Come on.

*(Mimi and Jones exit.*

*Almost immediately they come backing on.*
*Orry enters pointing his gun at them.)*

MIMI:  *(To herself.)* Where are all the black people?

ORRY MAIN:  Identify yourself negress?

MIMI:  I'm Prissy one of Colonel Sanders' niggers. He sent me to fetch his 11 herbs and spices.

*(Mimi advances and grabs Orry's gun.*

*In the same moment he snatches the Mammy doll.)*

ORRY MAIN: Hoodoo Voodoo woman!

MIMI: Give that back!

*(Orry turns to run.*

*Mimi drops the gun and jumps on Orry's back.)*

ORRY MAIN: You aint gonna work your black magic on me.

*(Orry and Mimi fight for the doll and stumble off stage.*

*Jones follows.)*

ORRY MAIN *(O.S.)*: Help me Jones. Save me from the dark powers of Voodoo!

*(The sound of time moving forward.*

*The sound of Jones screaming.)*

HARRY: We are moving out.

*(The band wakes. Ad-libs: What's going on? OMFG...etc.*

*Harry grabs Orry's gun and tosses it to Vivian.*

*Jones runs screaming through the space.*

*Vivian sees Jones, she draws down on him, he runs off.)*

HARRY: Runaway slaves, we are leaving!

*(The band runs off.*

*The sound of time moving forward.*

*Anita runs on - speaking as she crosses the space.)*

ANITA: Jeremy's Big House.

*(2 thuds off. Retching. Then another thud.*

*Mimi enters, dragging Orry by the feet.)*

MIMI: Jeremy! Jer! Jer! Goddamn it, Jer where the fuck are you? *(She pulls the Mammy doll from her pocket. )* Okay Mammy, let me see if I can set you to the right - Wait. I can runaway. Wait - No. I have to go back and find Tubman. Wait. Why?

*(Anita pokes her head out.)*

ANITA: Destiny. Destiny. Destiny.

MIMI: Wait - I think it's my destiny.

*(Anita exits.)*

MIMI: Wait - Who am I talking to? *(Exiting.)* Mammy take me back in time.

*(Mimi exits.*

*The sound of time moving backwards.*

*Jeremy enters removing ear buds.)*

JEREMY: Mimi? Mimi - Hello? I was in the base-

*(Jeremy freezes when he sees Orry. He kneels down next to him.*

*Orry wakes. He retches. He looks up sees Jeremy.)*

ORRY MAIN: Maddox?

*(He scrambles to his feet. Jeremy rises.)*

ORRY MAIN: Who are you? Where am I?

*(Jeremy steps towards Orry.)*

ORRY MAIN: Stay back. Where am I? Don't come near me. Stay back!

*(Orry stumbles off stage. Jeremy follows after him.*

*The sound of time moving, then retching off stage.*

*Mimi stumbles on. Jones runs on in the opposite direction.*

*Jones sees Mimi and hauls ass the other way.)*

MIMI: Hey! Wait!

*(Mimi takes off after Jones.*

*Harry and the Band run across the space.*

*Anita brings up the rear of the column. She is having fun!*

*Orry stumbles on stage. He moves to the edge of the space.*

*Jeremy enters.)*

JEREMY: All the doors are on a time lock there's no way in or
  out.

*(Jeremy moves to him. He strokes Orry's face.)*

JEREMY: We're gonna have some fun.

*(Jeremy leads Orry out.*

*Mimi enters, again.*

*From the opposite direction Harry and the Band enter.*

*They see Mimi and stop.*

*Harry draws down on Mimi.*

*Jones peeks out from backstage, no one sees him.*

*A frozen moment.*

*Anita sprints across the space.)*

MIMI: Harriet Tubman?

HARRY: Maybe. What do you want?

MIMI: My name is Mimi and I am here to help you start a war.

HARRY: I already got one, darlin'.

*(They freeze.*

*A long beat.*

*Everyone unfreezes.)*

MIMI: I'm from the future.

*(Beat. They think on the statement. Someone giggles. It catches.*

*Beat. Everyone bust out in deep belly laughs.*

*Harry looks Mimi over. She shakes her head.*

*Harry exits. The Band exits, laughing.*

*Mimi follows them.)*

# REBEL YELL

*(Anita enters. A minor costume adjustment and she is glittering and ready to perform.)*

ANITA: I can't be faded. The present. Jeremy's big house. There is music.

*(Spot on Anita. She sings a cappella.)*

ANITA: I walked the walk for you, babe/A thousand miles for you

*(Orry enter crawling on his hands and knees. He moves in time to music. It is almost slow motion.)*

ANITA: I dried your tears of pain, babe/A million times for you

*(Jeremy enters. He holds a whip.)*

ANITA: I'd sell my soul for you, babe/For money to burn for you/I'd give you all and have none, babe

*(Jeremy places his foot on Orry's back and slowly pushes him to the ground.)*

ANITA: Just-a, just-a, just-a, just-a

*(As Anita hits the "just-a" section and with slow exaggerated motion.*

*Jeremy strikes Orry with the whip.*

*Orry screams but no sound comes out.)*

ANITA: To have you here by me because/In the midnight hour, she cried more, more, more/With a rebel yell, she cried more, more, more/ In the midnight hour, babe, more, more, more

*(Jeremy continues to beat Orry until he is curled up into a ball.*

*Jeremy knees down and cradles him.)*

ANITA: With a rebel yell, more, more, more/In the midnight hour, she cried more, more, more

JEREMY: With a rebel yell, he cried more, more, more/In the midnight hour, babe, more, more, more/With a rebel yell, more, more, more, more, more, more

## ENTER LAUGHING. EXIT AT GUN POINT.
## ENTER AGAIN.

*(Harry enters, the Band behind her, still laughing.*

*Mimi slinks in behind them.*

*The Band parts and surrounds Mimi and Harry.)*

MIMI: *(To the Band.)* It's not funny anymore.

*(Harry holds up her hand. The laughter dies down.)*

MIMI: I really need to talk you, Miss Tubman.

*(Harry circles Mimi, sizing her up.)*

HARRY: So, you steal things for a living?

MIMI: So do you.

*(The Band lets out an Oooooo!)*

MIMI: I am here to help you.

HARRY: Does it look like I need help?

MIMI: Not really. I know this is pretty effective for this time and place, but what if you could free everyone?

*(Harry looks hard at Mimi.*

*Harry gestures and Vivian peels off from the group and exits.)*

HARRY: You carrying?

MIMI: Yeah, how did you know?

HARRY: It's a gift. Draw down in that direction in 5-4-3-2-

*(Jones creeps in.*

*Harry and Mimi draws down on him.*

68

*He turns to run and Vivian has her rifle trained on him. Jones raises his hands.*

*Knox lunges at him. He is restrained by Maddox and Shilo.*

*Harry looks over Jones.)*

HARRY: Let's move.

*(They exit with the ladies escorting Jones out by gun point.*

*Mimi and Vivian enter.)*

MIMI: Holy shit that is awful.

VIVIAN: And he's one of the nice ones. Omigawd. My BFF Zara, she's owned by the Gables and their Overseer is so fat and this one time at a corn shucking-

MIMI: So much suffering. I feel it all. Like I'm connected. Since I've been here, it's like there's been this shift inside of me. I know I haven't been here that long, but it's like. *(Singing.)* Nobody knows da troubles Ies seen. Nobody knows but Jesus.

VIVIAN: Uh-huh. *(Indicating the gun.)* Can I see?

MIMI: Sure. Be careful. It's complicated technology you might not-

*(Vivian strips the gun and puts it back together.)*

MIMI: Be familiar with it.

VIVIAN: What's it's name?

MIMI: Thor.

VIVIAN: I'm calling mine Angelina.

MIMI: He's a Sig P-two-twenty-six. Standard lock breech short recoil 13 round mag...

*(They wander to the side examining the gun as Jones and Knox enter.)*

JONES: ...A bright blue light and then she was gone. I'm telling true.

KNOX: Dude, stops talking to me.

JONES: Call me Maynard.

*(Knox tries to get away from Jones, he follows him as Shilo and Maddox enter.)*

MADDOX: I am only concerned with one future.

SHILO: Our future Mr. Maddox?

MADDOX: Yes, Miss Shilo.

SHILO: Oh, Mr. Maddox. But what if this woman is not crazy?

VIVIAN: Imagine if we had guns like this?

SHILO: Oh we could kill up everyone! I mean free everyone.

KNOX: Vengeance would be ours.

SHILO: But who would lead us on such a quest?

*(Harry enters and Anita - dressed to suggest she is a Quaker farm wife. Maybe she has on a bonnet.*

*The Band and Mimi look at Harry. Then huddle up. Jones stands on the outside. He wiggles his way in and is pushed out. Wiggles in. Pushed out. He finally finds a spot.*

*Harry and Anita have a quite conversation.*

*Anita steps out and says:)*

ANITA: The farm of the good Reverend Charles Ruben and his wife. One days walk from the Mason Dixon line. It is dawn.

HARRY: *(To Anita)* We thank thee for thy hospitality.

*(Anita nods and exits.)*

HARRY: *(Turning to the Group.)* These good Quakers folks are letting us use their barn-

*(Someone in the huddle clears their throat.*

*The Band quickly silence their conversation and form a line.*

*Mimi checks for her gun. She looks to Vivian. Vivian looks to Maddox. Maddox to Shilo. Shilo to Knox. Knox to Jones.*

*Jones to - No one is there. Jones looks down. He has the gun in his hand.*

*Knox snatch it from him. Shilo takes it from Knox. She passes to Maddox. Maddox to Vivian. Vivian to Mimi. She holsters her weapon.)*

HARRY: What?

MADDOX: General, what is your opinion on guns? Guns from, ahem, the future.

HARRY: Really? This how you wanna behave when you are running for your lives? Really? Okay. Let's talk guns. Take this one for example.

*(Harry draws down on the Band.)*

HARRY: In a really grim future this one here kills everyone in this barn. Listen up. You people are getting to freedom. If I have to drag your corpses there, so be it. But no one and nothing is gonna get in my way. Conversation over. Chow and sleep. We leave at night fall. Vivian, you got first watch and guard the prisoner. *(To Mimi.)* You with me. Let's here this plan of yours. Move. *(As they exit.)* What are you trying to do? What is wrong with you?

*(Everyone exits except for Vivian and Jones.)*

# KEEP ON LOVING YOU

*(Vivian holds her rifle and looks out. Jones rocks the baby. He attempts to speak. Vivian shakes her head no.*

*Long Pause.*

*Jones hums to the baby. Vivian looks at him. He stops.*

*Pause.)*

JONES: Y'all don't have to hold me prisoner. I aint going back to the plantation. Mr. Scarlet aint a nice man. He hurt my feelings. He called me trash said I wasn't suppose to claim Malik.

VIVIAN: Who's Malik?

JONES: Our baby.

VIVIAN: What the hell kinda name is Malik?

JONES: I believe it's Arabic for king.

VIVIAN: It totally blows.

JONES: Well if you were so concerned about what to call Malik. You should have named him. I wasn't about keep calling my boy What's-his-name. *(Pause. To Malik.)* Aint mommy pretty when she knows daddy's right. Aint mommy pretty with her big ole gun. She's brave. You have a brave mommy. *(Pause.)* So, where you headed once you get to freedom?

VIVIAN: No, Maynard.

JONES: I would like Malik to know his mother.

VIVIAN: I hate that name.

JONES: So I figured where you go...

VIVIAN: That's not going to happen.

72

JONES: Malik needs a mommy. It is not his fault that his daddy is an asshole. What I did to you was unspeakable. I see that. *(Pause.)* I'm sorry. I have to break character for a moment and say it hurts playing a rapist and racist. I understand that men like that existed, still exist, but I wanted to be clear that this is not who I am. This character is not *[Actor's name]*. *[Actor's name]* doesn't see color. I also want to say that I am honored to be a part of this production. Slavery and the institutional racism that it engendered, that lingers is a blight on our nation and our souls. The contribution of African-American women to American history and culture has long been ignored and diminished. As a White American I urge all my white brothers and sisters to stand against racism, to search our hearts, to reach out to people of color-

VIVIAN: Dude, this so aint about you.

JONES: I know but I feel so bad.

VIVIAN: Deal with your guilt on your own time, brother man. And thanks for acknowledging the issue.

JONES: Word. I'll buy you a drink at *[Local bar where the actors been drinking]*.

VIVIAN: Sweet. Shall we continue?

JONES: Malik needs a mommy. It is not his fault that his daddy is an asshole. What I did to you was unspeakable. I see that.

VIVIAN: You're just figuring this out now?

JONES: No. I knew it was wrong when I did it. But I wanted you. And I knew you couldn't do nothing to stop me.

VIVIAN: I can stop you now.

JONES: And it would serve me right. I hate myself for what I did to you.

VIVIAN: Finally something we can agree on.

JONES: I am sorry from the bottom of my soul.

VIVIAN: I don't want your Goddamn apologies. I want you leave me alone. I want you to take that baby and go far away from me.

JONES: You aint got any tender feeling for our boy?

*(Vivian doesn't say anything.)*

JONES: That's my fault.

VIVIAN: Yeah it is.

JONES: I know I can't never make it right. I know that. But, I love our, son. I am gonna raise him to be a good man. *(Beat.)* Can I ask you for a favor?

VIVIAN: What else can I possibly give you?

JONES: *(Smiling, lewdly.)* Well...

VIVIAN: Get out.

JONES: I'm sorry. I can't help it.

VIVIAN: You better work on it. What is the favor?

JONES: Please keep your brother from killing me.

VIVIAN: You die, whose gonna raise the baby, right?

JONES: I was hoping you'd see it that way.

VIVIAN: I'll see what I can do.

JONES: What you gonna do when you reach freedom?

VIVIAN: I dunno.

JONES: You'll figure something out. You're real strong. Real strong. I admire that about you.

VIVIAN: I'd like to do more of this. Traveling. Making my way in the world by my wits and my gun. *(Beat.)* This is the farthest from home I've ever been.

JONES: I went to Baltimore once. It was big. Lots of tall ships. It scared me.

*(Vivian looks out. Jones rocks Malik. He begins to sing to him, softly.)*

JONES: *(Singing.)* And I meant every word I said/ when I said that I love you I meant that I'd love you forever./ And I'm gonna keep on loving you./ Cuz it's the only thing I wanna do I don't wanna sleep...

*(Knox enter. He looks menacingly at Jones.)*

# SIGN

*(Mimi and Harry enter.)*

HARRY: I had never been more nervous, more cautious, more jumpy. I wish I had worn a dress, but it was safer to travel as a man and my disguise was good. I imagined the laughter when the door opened and I took off my hat. 2 years. I had made it north and come back a few times always fighting the itch to go down that road. And there I was standing on it and all I wanted to do was run the other way. I could see the cabin. The lamp was burning. That was a good sign. Not too much moon another good sign. No black outs. I never had an easier trip. I crept up to the back door and pressed my ear to it, my heart knocking against the wood. Footsteps. Would my heart announce my presence? I got myself together and went to the front and knocked. A blast of warm, the smell of something good cooking. The light of a lamp surrounding him. "What you want?" He's gruff, he don't know it's me. I throw off my hat. "John, it's me, Harriet. I've come back to take you to freedom." Why hasn't he opened the door? Why hasn't he opened his arms? He looks me over. I'm ready to jump into him. His voice lowers. "What you want?" "John, it's me. It's Harriet." But I don't say that. I just stare over his shoulder as she walks towards us. Actually she glides. It's like she's the one given off the light and warmth in the cabin. Her hand is smooth on his arm. Her voice soft with unmistakable ownership. "John, who's this?" He had a new wife.

MIMI: Nigga, what?

HARRY: *(She sits.)* He had a new wife.

MIMI: Are you serious? This what you get for helping people? I don't understand. You traveled like 100 miles-

HARRY: 150-

MIMI: One hundred and fifty fucking miles to free him.

HARRY: Technically he was already "free." But yeah. Funny the new wife wanted to go with me.

MIMI: Was she pretty?

HARRY: You mean was she prettier than me?

MIMI: That's not what I meant.

HARRY: Yes she was.

MIMI: You should have taken her and left her pretty ass in the woods.

HARRY: John wouldn't have it. Just like when I wanted to run he threatened to tell the man. I would have guided her to freedom. It wasn't her fault that John didn't love me anymore. Maybe some of us weren't made for love.

MIMI: That's depressing.

HARRY: You got a man?

MIMI: No.

HARRY: I liked being married. I loved being in love. Being loved.

MIMI: I am trippin. You are Harriet Tubman you are noble brave and true.

HARRY: And alone. *(Beat.)* I know why you're here.

MIMI: Yeah?

HARRY: Yes. I've been praying on this problem that's been eating at my heart. Praying for the Lord to give me sign. You're here to let me know it's okay to quit.

MIMI: Quit what?

HARRY: Quit this.

MIMI: This this?

HARRY: Yes.

MIMI: No.

HARRY: Yes.

MIMI: No.

HARRY: I'm through this is gonna be my last trip North.

MIMI: No. Why?

HARRY: Look, I really like my job, helping people, doing God's work, the action, it's really incredible. But without somebody to love...And I just can't be in the same state as John anymore.

MIMI: You'll get over it.

HARRY: I'm gonna get these folks North, then I'm off to Canada.

MIMI: You can't give up.

HARRY: Maybe England. I think an ocean between us is a suitable distance. I really liked being married.

MIMI: You'll find someone else.

HARRY: I'm gonna be alone forever.

MIMI: Dude, I'm from the future.

HARRY: So you know for sure that I get another husband?

MIMI: Well...

HARRY: Don't lie to me.

MIMI: You're Harriet Tubman, Moses of her people. I played you in my third grade school play. You are a hero. An icon. A legend.

HARRY: A woman alone. Who will die alone. Who no one will ever love. Unlovable.

MIMI: I am not going to dignify that pitiful bullshit with a response. You don't quit. Just accept it.

HARRY: I got a sleeping sickness and when I black out the Lord gives me vision. Last time I was out I saw you, walking through the woods leading folks. And I take that to mean that the Lord has found his self another vessel.

MIMI: I am not a sign. God has not sent me. No God! No! I am here with a proposal from my cousin. Look. I think the plan is insane and will fail. Might fail. I dunno. I am kinda on the fence about its veracity and my whole part in the scheme. I am sure it will alter the course of history forever. But hear me out.

HARRY: I don't need to.

MIMI: So, you're in? Without hearing the proposal?

HARRY: I'm done. I'm convinced that you are the sign that I have been waiting for. This will be my last mission. Praise Jesus.

*(Harry exits.)*

MIMI: No. Wait!

*(Anita sticks her head out from back stage.)*

ANITA: Destiny. Destiny. Destiny.

*(Mimi looks around. Is she hearing things? Mimi exits after Harry.)*

# OUT OF THE BLUE

*(Anita enters.)*

ANITA: Montage.

*(Out of the Blue by Debbie Gibson - Karaoke version begins to play.*

*Maddox and Shilo waltz on. They take a turn around the space.*

*Maddox and Shilo second go round, Knox and Jones enter from the opposite side.*

*Knox and Jones cross towards each other and meet in the center as Maddox and Shilo dance around them.*

*Knox and Jones circle each other as the following dialogue occurs.)*

KNOX: I'm gonna kill you now, Joney.

JONES: My day of reckoning, I reckon.

KNOX: My family honor will be restored.

JONES: May I have a moment to talk you out of it?

KNOX: The only thing I wanna here from you is how you want to die.

JONES: Quickly and not in front of my boy.

*(Jones holds out Malik. Knox stops and looks at the baby.)*

KNOX: He's got my mama's chin.

JONES: Thems my paw-paws eyebrows.

*(Knox takes the baby.)*

KNOX: When I hold him out and squint. He looks just like me. *(Beat.)* Ah, shit.

*(Jones reaches out for the baby. Knox grabs his arms.*

*They hold each other baby between them.*

*They begin to waltz around the stage with Maddox and Shilo.)*

ANITA: Spin. Spin. To the Present.

*(The 2 couples make a loop on the second go around...*

*Orry and Jeremy enter waltzing. Orry cries, softly. Jeremy sighs.)*

JEREMY: Having a slave is suppose to be fun. You are no fun. If I could beat you to death and buy another just like you I would.

*(The couples dance in a wide circle.)*

ANITA: Spin. Months later.

ORRY MAIN: Mercy. We lost? What happens after the war?

JEREMY: The history lesson is over for today. It is nice to see you in a better mood.

ORRY MAIN: That's cuz, I now know how to keep you from beating me.

*(The 4 couples circle the space.)*

ANITA: Spin. Months later.

JEREMY: I am afraid Mimi is dead and you can never going home. But I am freeing you. Youes free Orry.

ORRY MAIN: I don't want to go home. I really like the hot water on tap you got here. And I like you.

JEREMY: You do?

ORRY MAIN: That don't make you happy?

JEREMY: It does.

ORRY MAIN: They why aren't you smiling?

JEREMY: I failed. I was gonna rule the world. My dream is over.

ORRY MAIN: Jeremy Chad Washington. If I have learned anything these past 6 months it is that you are a brilliant, determined, splendid black man, who can do what ever he sets his mind to. So, baby if you want to rule the world, then rule the world.

JEREMY: What did I do to deserve you?

ORRY MAIN: Accidentally kidnap me from my time and I am so happy that you did.

*(They kiss.)*

ANITA: Spin. Spin. Spin. Back to the past.

*(Harry and Mimi enter.*

*The couples continue to dance in the background.)*

HARRY: Am I cool enough to enjoy the strawberry? Strawberries give me a rash.

MIMI: It's a metaphor.

HARRY: Yeah. I get it. I also get that your cousin thought I was some dumb hayseed nigga that could be easily led with the promise of some shiny guns. Guess the joke's on him cuz I aint the one.

*(Couples circle the space.)*

HARRY: Okay sell it to me.

MIMI: Working with you made me realize this job isn't about me.

HARRY: Right, it's about me.

MIMI: No. It's about Shilo and Vivian, Maddox and Knox. About all the folks like them. We gotta chance to make centuries of wrongs right. To make this country live up to it's founding principles: that all men are created equal.

*(Harry blacks out.)*

MIMI: We can make this nation great. Skip all horrors of Jim Crow and Speedy Gonzales straight into Justice Sotomayor, Kamala D. Harris and Robin Thicke. America, Harry, she's my strawberry and with or without you I am gonna eat her. Are you in?

*(Vivian enters. She begins to dance with her rifle.*

*Anita dances.)*

MIMI: Harry? Harry?

*(The couples circle the space.)*

# FREEDOM '58

*(The dancing continues around Harry.)*

HARRY: *(Still sleeping.)* Take the bandana!

*(Harry bolts awake.)*

HARRY: What the Sam Hell is going on here?

*(The dancing stops.*

*Orry and Jeremy exit.*

*Anita exits.)*

SHILO: The light through the barn's beams was so enchanting.

MADDOX: Nature and love conspire to let the joy in one's soul overflow.

HARRY: Yeah, aint love grand. Saddle up we are Oscar Mike in 5.

VIVIAN: *(To Knox.)* You've made up with him?

KNOX: Kinda sort of.

JONES: *(To Mimi)* Aint he the most beautiful child?

KNOX: I figured since you forgave him.

MIMI: *(To Jones.)* He's okay.

VIVIAN: I didn't forgive him.

JONES: Black babies are the prettiest babies. Even though Malik is only half, he's 100% beautiful.

VIVIAN: I just don't want to blow his face off.

MIMI: *(To Jones.)* Please stop talking to me. *(To Harry.)* I can't believe your taking him *(Indicating Jones.)* with you?

HARRY: I free slaves, baby.

VIVIAN: You are so cool.

HARRY: Everyone gather round. This is the final push. You will see tomorrow's sun rise with free eyes. Take a knee. Dear Lord. Thank you for getting us this far. Please continue to protect us on our journey. And Lord all powerful merciful Lord thank you for showing me the sign to my personal freedom. I am forever your righteous servant. Ah-

MIMI: Hi. God. Goddess. Universe. Whatever. I'm not sure I believe in you, but I'm in a tight spot. Please help me convince someone that they are being stupid and will condemn a bunch of people to the horrors of chattel slavery forever, if they do what they are thinking about doing. Help me and I will totally owe you forever. I pinky swear. Ah-

KNOX: God please get me safely to Mexico and help me find a job there. Ah-

VIVIAN: God thanks for restraining me when I wanted to kill Maynard. And thanks for making him want to take Whats-his-name. And thank you for the General. For her bravery and ultra-coolness. And thanks for my rifle. May I shoot straight and true. Ah-

MADDOX: Lord Jehovah, please carry me and my beloved Shilo safely from these shores of savagery to the civilized clime of Europe. Ah-

SHILO: Sweet baby Jesus, thank you for my Maddox-

JONES: Lord. Thank you. Thank you for allowing me and Malik to find these good folks. Thank you Lord for filling their hearts with forgiveness and mercy. And Lord thank you for washing the poison of hatred from my heart. Lord I was so lost, so lost. But did you forsake me? Did you turn your back on me? Did you let me drown in the bitter waters of bigotry and evil? No! You dried my clothes! You gave me a clean town and--

HARRY: Uh, yeah. Amen, everyone.

MIMI: Good luck, people. I am heading back to the future.

*(Vivian and Mimi do an elaborate soul hand shake.)*

VIVIAN: Right on, sistah.

MIMI: Watch your back, mama.

*(Harry nods and Vivian ushers the band out.)*

HARRY: I figured out an alternative to your plan. Tell your cousin he should give those guns to John Brown. I can put y'all in contact. He'd definitely be interested in some weaponry and that nigga is down for whatever and ready to roll.

MIMI: Don't try to sell me on Brown. It's gotta be you. So, don't quit. *(Taking Harry by the shoulders.)* You hear me. I am coming back. We can do this Harry. I can do this. I won't let you down. Please don't give up. Have some faith. You are the one good thing that I got. I won't let you down. Please don't give up. I really love you to stick around.

HARRY: Why are you touching me?

MIMI: *(Letting her go.)* Sorry.

HARRY: I'll do it.

MIMI: Seriously?

HARRY: Yeah.

MIMI: For real?

HARRY: Yes.

MIMI: Why? You didn't have ones of those mystical vision things when you were out?

HARRY: No. I didn't have one of those. Best not to question. Just let the series of events wash over you.

ANITA: *(Either offstage or poking her head out.)* Destiny.

HARRY:  Get going.

MIMI:  Wait. Where am I gonna meet you?

HARRY:  You'll find me.

MIMI:  How?

ANITA:  Destiny.

HARRY:  Fly fly little Mimi. See you soon.

*(Harry exit.)*

ANITA:  Destiny. Destiny. Destin-

MIMI:  Oh for fuck sake. I hear you.

*(Mimi exits.*

*Moments later. Harry and The Band roll in.*

*They walk through the space in an elaborate complex pattern.*

*Harry stops. She takes a dramatic step over an imaginary line. Everyone follows suit.)*

HARRY:  Welcome to freedom.

KNOX:  This is it?

HARRY:  Yeah.

SHILO:  We're free?

MADDOX:  Delightful.

HARRY:  Yes.

KNOX:  Feels a little anti-climatic. Anyone else having that sensation? Like maybe freedom isn't a place but a feeling. A feeling that we've always carried within us.

*(Vivian and Knox look at each other.)*

KNOX:  Naw

VIVIAN: Naw

*(Knox and Vivian embrace.*

*Shilo joins in. Then Maddox.*
*They all jump up and down. YAY!*

*Jones stand outside the circle and jumps with them.)*

HARRY: Listen up. Town is 2 miles yonder. 10 miles beyond
that is Philly. There you can catch trains to New York, West
or Canada. We're gonna split up now. When you reach
town keep a low profile. Slave catchers are everywhere.
And of course you've never seen me.

SHILO: *(Embracing Harry.)* Oh General! Oh General! Oh
General!

HARRY: Yes. Your welcome. Please release me.

MADDOX: Madame, my gratitude cannot be measured. I hope
a humble and deep felt thank you is sufficient.

HARRY: It is, sir.

MADDOX: *(Bows.)* General.

*(Maddox and Shilo embrace.*

*They shake hand with Vivian and Knox.*

*They ignore Jones.)*

MADDOX: Miss Shilo.

SHILO: Yes, Mr. Maddox.

*(They take each others hand.*

*Shilo and Maddox pose as if taking a prom picture.*

*Everyone freezes.*

*Anita enters.)*

ANITA: Shilo Ashley Steward and Maddox Lee Brown move to Paris. Maddox studies music. He composes a popular chamber piece called Ballade de Moise. Shilo opens Shilo's Apothecary Pastry Cafe on Rue Saint Rustigio. Her petite creme pieds were a comfort to many workers during the Paris Commune. The shop remains open to this day.

*(Everyone unfreezes.*

*Maddox and Shilo exit.)*

KNOX: I'm sorry, I was such a pain.

HARRY: There's always one. Go be a hero.

JONES: Miss General, ma'am. Thanks you for giving my boy a fresh start.

HARRY: You just make sure he finishes.

VIVIAN: General, sir.

HARRY: Vivian.

VIVIAN: Meet you in Philly?

HARRY: I won't let you down. Give Jones the rifle while you're in town. Folks might not take to a black woman with a gun.

*(Jones reaches for the gun. Vivian pulls away.)*

VIVIAN: If they want it they can pry it from my cold dead hands.

HARRY: That's an order.

*(Vivian tosses the gun to Jones.*

*Vivian, Knox and Jones start to exit.*

*Vivian turns.)*

VIVIAN: General.

*(Vivian gives Harry a crisp salute. Harry returns a casual one and freezes.*

*Vivian, Knox and Jones pose for a grim 19th century family photo.)*

ANITA:  Knox Joseph Pitt makes it west. He works and saves and eventually purchases land. He builds Rancho Pitt in Vera Cruz and becomes the most successful vaquero in all of Mexico. Maynard Jones works at Rancho Pitt and raises his son. He never marries. He lives long enough to see Malik become a rancher and the father of three girls.

*(Knox, Jones and Malik exit.)*

ANITA:  Vivian Madonna Pitt, disguises herself as a man and joins the army. After the war she goes west with the US 10th Calvary. Disgusted by the army's policy towards Native Americans, she deserts and forms a gang. The legend of the black woman bandit, So Raven, haunts the west for 25 years, then Raven and her gang vanish. Some say she was caught, some say she was killed. And some say she retired to Vera Cruz a wealthy woman.

*(Vivian exits.)*

# BACK TO THE FUTURE 2

ANITA: Interior. Jeremy's big house. The present.

*(Orry and Jeremy waltz on.)*

ORRY MAIN: You always bring that up when I am right.

JEREMY: But you did own slaves.

ORRY MAIN: You held me captive.

JEREMY: I freed you.

ORRY MAIN: The point is you promised for our anniversary we'd go somewhere warm with nice blue water. You promised, Daddy.

JEREMY: Don't use sex as a weapon it's distasteful.

ORRY MAIN: I'm being flirtatious.

*(Anita exits.)*

JEREMY: The Caribbean will be ghastly this time of year. Malta? Greece? We can island hop.

ORRY MAIN: I can sail a sloop.

JEREMY: Oh my 19th century man.

ORRY MAIN: Jeremy.

JEREMY: Yes, Orry.

ORRY MAIN: I lo-

*(The sound of time moving forward.)*

ORRY MAIN: What the sam hell was that?

*(The sound of retching.)*

JEREMY: No.

*(They exit towards the sound of the noise.*

*Mimi stumbles on.*

*Jeremy and Orry follow.)*

MIMI:  Dude, you sent me back to the wrong time and state.

JEREMY:  So you didn't find Tubman?

MIMI:  I found her. Only it was before the war. She was on a mission taking folks north. I was with her a couple days. *(Notices Orry and going after him.)* You!

JEREMY:  May I present to you. Mr. Orry Main, my beloved gentleman.

MIMI:  I need those guns, man. Harry is waiting.

JEREMY:  Honey, you've been gone a year.

MIMI:  What?

ORRY MAIN:  We just celebrated our anniversary.

MIMI:  What?

JEREMY:  When you didn't come back I thought the war had got you. So I had to form a new plan. Meeting Orry made me re-examine my ideas around race and slavery and all that. And I came to the conclusion what I was really after was power.

ORRY MAIN:  Yes.

JEREMY:  Pure naked power. Race doesn't matter. Jeremy does not see color anymore.

MIMI:  Whatever. I need those guns. Harry is waiting on me.

JEREMY:  I'm over the Harriet thing. I gave the guns to Ronnie, Bobby, Ricky and Mike and sent them on a few errands through time.

ORRY MAIN: We got pirate's booty.

JEREMY: Russian crown jewels.

MIMI: I have to go back! Tubman took me as sign from God telling her it was okay to quit taking the enslaved north.

JEREMY: OMFG! What did you do to Moses?!

MIMI: It wasn't me, dude. She's heartbroken. She left her husband the first time she ran. A year later she went back to get him and he had another wife.

ORRY MAIN: Nigga, what?

JEREMY: No.

ORRY MAIN: I'm sorry. I thought I used it in the right context.

JEREMY: You did baby and the inflection was perfect. I should be more patience. You're still learning.

MIMI: Guns! Jeremy, I need guns! And I need you to send me back in time. NOW!

JEREMY: Okay. Keep your panties on. Take all the guns you need.

MIMI: You're not going to fight me on this?

JEREMY: No. Love has changed my heart.

MIMI: Love, huh? It's that simple?

ORRY MAIN: Oh, grurl, it's anything but simple. But it is love.

JEREMY: Let me check Mammy. *(Jeremy tinkers with Mammy.)* Okay. Off you go. Orry will get you some guns. Oh, sorry I blackmailed you into traveling back in time.

MIMI: That's okay. I have been profoundly changed.

JEREMY:  Good for you. When you get back the 3 of us will have dinner.

MIMI:  I'd like that.

*(Mimi and Orry exit.)*

JEREMY:  Orry, baby, put down towels.

MIMI *(O.S.)*:  Oh shit! This set this for the Civil War?! Noooo-

*(The sound of time moving backwards.*

*Orry enters.  He grabs Jeremy and dips him.)*

ORRY MAIN:  I gave her the last of the M60s.

JEREMY:  That's fine. What was she going on about?

*(As they waltz off.)*

ORRY MAIN:  I dunno something about the Civil War.

JEREMY:  Let's go buy a sloop.

# DON'T CALL IT A COME BACK.

*(Anita enters - she is dressed for the Civil War. (Maybe Scarlet O'Haraesque. Or in Confederate solider chic.))*

ANITA:   June 1863, South Carolina. The Civil War. War sounds. Horses, wagon wheels squeaking, the crack of rile fire, men screaming, dying. War. War. War.

*(The sound of time moving backwards, then retching.*

*Harry and Vivian run on shooting.*

*Anita shrieks and runs out.*

*Harry and Vivian take cover. Vivian takes aim)*

HARRY:   You got 'em?

VIVIAN:   Yeah. Three near the tree.

HARRY:   Take 'em.

*(Vivian fires three shots. Faint screams heard.*

*Mimi stumbles on behind Vivian and Harry. They turn, guns drawn.)*

MIMI:   Hey! Fuck! I'm a friendly.

HARRY:   Hello Mimi.

MIMI:   Harry? Vivian? I can't believe I found you. I went to the wrong time, again. I thought for sure you would have quit. Oh Harry! I got the guns-

*(Gunfire. Harry tackles Mimi to the ground.)*

HARRY:   You okay?

MIMI:   Yeah. You?

VIVIAN:   I'm so coming for you Rebel Cracker Dog!

*(Vivian scampers off to another part of the space engaging the enemy.*

*Mimi take off the M60 strapped to her and hands it to Harry.)*

MIMI:  Here. I have more I stashed.

HARRY:  I lied to you.

MIMI:  Why? When?

HARRY:  God gave me another vision.

MIMI:  Oh, shit.

HARRY:  Don't worry. This vision was about me. I was here. I saw this.

*(Harry doubles over.)*

MIMI:  Are you hit?

HARRY:  Yes.

MIMI:  No.

HARRY:  Yes.

MIMI:  No.

HARRY:  Stop doing that. I am hit. And it hurts.

MIMI:  Fuck!  In In In your vision-

HARRY:  Yeah I die.

MIMI:  Shit. I shouldn't have come back.

HARRY:  It's not your fault.

MIMI:  In your vision did you see me holding your hand. Me holding back tears.

HARRY:  Don't go soft on me.

MIMI:  Please, Harry hang on.  You've gonna be so fucking famous for helping people. I Googled you.

HARRY:  I don't know what that is. God is great. He said you'd be my Moses. That you'd know what to do.

MIMI:  About what?

HARRY:  That I don't need to worry anymore. It's up to you now, Mimi.

MIMI:  What's up to me?

HARRY:  It's all on you. I just gotta close my eyes-

MIMI:  No. No. What's on me?

HARRY:  I'm dying. Stop playing dumb.

MIMI:  I aint playin'.

HARRY:  I'm coming home Lord.

MIMI:  No. Wait. Just tell me what I am suppose to do?

*(Harry reaches up and pulls Mimi to her.)*

HARRY:  Trust yourself. Look inside for the answer. This is your des-tin-neee.

*(Harry goes limp.)*

MIMI:  No. No. No. I don't know what to do? Harry! Don't you give up on me! Harry! Tell me what I am suppose to do.

*(Mimi begins to weep over Harry's body.*

*Harry inhales sharply. She rips the bandana off of her head and shoves it into Mimi's hands.)*

HARRY:  Take the bandana. Become the General. Get your shit together. Don't fuck it up.

*(Harry dies.)*

MIMI: Harry? Harry? Harry. I love you.

*(Harry pops back up.)*

HARRY: I love you too.

*(Harry dies, again.)*

MIMI: Noooooooooooo!

*(Vivian runs over.)*

VIVIAN: General? General! General!

*(Vivian sobs over Harry's body.)*

MIMI: Vivian. Go get a shovel and a blanket. Vivian!

VIVIAN: The General is dead.

*(Mimi grabs Vivian.)*

MIMI: The General is not dead.

*(Mimi puts on the bandana.)*

MIMI: The General is not dead. Understand?

VIVIAN: Yes, sir.

*(Vivian kneels and kisses Harry. She rises and salutes Mimi.*

*Vivian exits.*

*Mimi picks up the M60. She freezes.*

*Anita enters. Perhaps another costume change? Maybe the ensemble from the opening?)*

ANITA:  Harriet Tubman made 20 trips to the south and brought 300 enslaved people to freedom. Including her entire family. The bounty on her head was 40,000 dollars. During the Civil War Harry frees over 700 people. 2 years after the war ends Harry's first husband John was found dead in Maryland. April 14, 1865 Harry is at the Ford's

Theatre. A grateful president puts Harry in charge of Reconstruction. With an abundance of weaponry and allies both black and white Harry transform the southern United States into a haven for free thinking, free love, social, racial and gender equality. In 1882 the South invades the North. In 1890, Harriet Tubman is elected President of the United States of America. In 1899, she mysteriously disappears from the oval office, never to be heard from again.

*(Mimi unfreezes. Lock and load.*

*Mimi runs off giving a war cry.)*

ANITA: Harry &the Thief. With *(Actor's name.)* as Mimi, the thief.

*(Mimi enters and bows.*

*As their names are called each company member enters and bows.)*

ANITA: *(Actor's name.)* as Jeremy, the mad scientist. *(Actor's name.)* as Orry Main Scarlet. *(Actor's name.)* as Maddox. *(Actor's name.)* as Shilo. *(Actor's name.)* as Knox. *(Actor's name.)* as Jones. *(Actor's name.)* as Vivian. And *(Actor's name.)* as Harriet Tubman.

*(Long beat.*

*The house lights do not come up.*

*Enter Jeremy and Mimi from opposite sides of the space.)*

JEREMY: I have another job for you.

*(Enter Orry.)*

ORRY MAIN: I can't believe I lived in this century it's so dirty.

MIMI: I can't leave to go on one your crazy quest for booty. I'm the president. The country needs me.

JEREMY: Yes she do. In the year 2095, America needs you. The earth needs you. The Galactic Alliance needs you.

ORRY MAIN: The lizard people have taken over the world and have enslaved all of humanity. It's so terrible. We barely made it out.

JEREMY: And we have only 24 hours to stop them before they blow up the earth. We've brought you some help.

*(Enter Harry.)*

MIMI: Harry!

HARRY: Hey girl.

MIMI: But you're-

HARRY: An angel, yes. The fate of the world is on the line but I can't do it alone. Whatda say?

MIMI: I always wanted a pair of lizard skin pumps.

HARRY: Then let's roll.

*(Another of cool ass tableaux.)*

ANITA: Harry & the Thief 2: Scales of Justice. Summer 2016.

**END OF PLAY**

# NOTES

Made in the USA
Middletown, DE
20 September 2020